Growing Up
Is Optional

Rediscover the Joy of Play

GAIL MOORE

BALBOA.
PRESS

A DIVISION OF HAY HOUSE

Balboa Press books may be ordered through booksellers or by contacting:

Balboa Press
A Division of Hay House
1663 Liberty Drive
Bloomington, IN 47403
www.balboapress.com
1 (877) 407-4847

Printed in the United States of America.

ISBN: 978-1-4525-9228-2 (sc)
ISBN: 978-1-4525-9229-9 (e)

Balboa Press rev. date: 02/19/2014

Dedication

To Phil, my wonderful, loving, supportive husband and best friend.

Our children Kirsty, Iain and Liam who light up our lives and go along with all our mad ideas, even though they think we are crazy!

I love you all.

"But I don't want to go among mad people," Alice remarked.
"Oh, you can't help that," said the Cat: "we're all mad here. I'm mad. You're mad."
"How do you know I'm mad?" said Alice.
"You must be," said the Cat, or you wouldn't have come here."

- Lewis Carroll, Alice in Wonderland.

Once upon a time you were open to everything.

There was so much to see and explore.

You believed you could be and do anything you wanted.

When being brave and fearless was what you would do in a typical day.

You didn't need anyone to tell you how wonderful and perfect you were because you knew it already.

Remember when your big brother was your hero and you wanted to protect your little sister. A thunderstorm wasn't going to spoil your day but made it more exciting. You didn't have an agenda and just played for the sake of playing. You had the biggest fight in the world but a short time later were friends again.

How you jumped out of bed in the morning, excited for the day ahead. You loved unconditionally and didn't make judgments about people but just accepted them the way they were.

That childlike state is your natural state.

Confident, sure of your abilities, not afraid of failing because you know with practice and determination you'll get it right, adventurous and willing to embrace new experiences, fun loving and full of energy.

Keeping that childlike state is the fountain of youth.

You look and feel younger when you have a zest for life. A happy personality, nice smile and twinkle in your eye can take years of you and as research shows help you to live longer.

You are also more able to deal with any of life's challenges when you have a happier outlook as you have a different perspective on difficult situations when you're in a good mood compared to a bad mood.

Don't you just feel how your energy levels lower as you think of boring things and rise as you think of fun and happy things?

"All work and no play makes Jack a very dull boy."

- proverb

You didn't come to this life to sit on your bum, you came for the adventure. Life is all about growth and expansion.

Your children are reminding you.

Your pets are reminding you.

Your inner child is reminding you or he/she wouldn't have drawn you to this book.

"What do most Nobel Laureates, innovative entrepreneurs, artists and performers, well-adjusted children, happy couples and families, and 'the most successfully adapted mammals' have in common? They play enthusiastically through their lives.

Play refreshes a long-term adult-adult relationship; some of the hallmarks of its refreshing oxygenating action are: humour, the enjoyment of novelty, the capacity to share a light-hearted sense of the world's ironies, the enjoyment of mutual storytelling, the capacity to openly divulge imagination and fantasies.

These playful communications and interactions, when nourished, produce a climate for easy connection and deepening more rewarding relationship – true intimacy."

- Stuart Brown, The National Institute for Play

"In every real man, a child is hidden that wants to play."

- Friedrich Nietzsche

Say to yourself throughout the day "what can I do to have more fun and laughter?"

And when you find yourself having fun, laughing, being happy, then acknowledge it and tell yourself you want to feel like this more often. This is my natural state of being and I love it.

"I am a happier person when I have fun; people want to be with me,
I am fun to be around, I feel better,
I look better, I have more patience,
I see things differently, I feel energised.
It feels good to feel good,
I love having fun.
Each day I'm going to find ways to bring some
fun and laughter into my life.
I am interested to see what happens in my life when I have more fun.
It doesn't have to be anything big
I could just skip around this room or I could
put on a great song, and dance.
I love having fun!"

- Gail Moore

If a friend or relative could do with being cheered up then take them to the park, seaside or zoo.

Is someone in hospital? Take a board game or playing cards and sit and play with them.

Do your children spend all day in their rooms? Take them swimming or for a bike ride. Help them to make their own vision board and spend quality time together cutting out pictures from magazines and talking about what they'd like to be, do and have in their life.

When you think of ways to bring fun and joy into other people's lives, you automatically bring more into your own!

*"Happiness is the meaning
and the purpose
Of life, the whole aim and end
Of human existence."*

- Aristotle

Do it for that child within you, waiting patiently to come out and play. That part of you that knows "Growing up is optional."

Go on I dare you!

Have more fun and games in your life and just see what happens.

What have you got to lose?

Tell some jokes

"Everyone should be able to do one card trick, tell two jokes, and recite three poems, in case they are ever trapped in an elevator."
- Lemony Snicker, Horseradish: Bitter Truths You Can't Avoid

Laughter is good for you. It's good medicine because it not only lightens your mood and relaxes you but has many health benefits including lowering stress, boosting the immune system and releasing endorphins, the body's natural feel good chemicals.

Humour in any relationship strengthens the bond and brings you closer together making it easier to express your feelings and overcome any difficulties.

I could go on about all the benefits of laughter but you probably know it yourself anyway, so have a good chuckle to yourself and put a smile on someone's face.

Buy a joke book or look online for some jokes. Ask family and friends if they have any favourite jokes.

Watch your favourite comedian's DVD or go and see their live show.

"Knock, knock."	"Knock, knock."
"Who's there?"	"Who's there?"
"Cows go."	"Catch."
"Cows go who?"	"Catch who?"
"No! Cows go moo."	"God bless you."

My husband and I were in a bookshop looking in the humour section, giggling at some of the books like naughty school children. At one point Phil was laughing so much he had tears running down his face and could only point at what was funny as he couldn't speak.

"A day without laughter is a day wasted."

- Charlie Chaplin

Throw stones in the water

"Enjoy life. There's plenty of time to be dead."
- Hans Christian Andersen

Being in nature, especially near water has a relaxing and calming effect on the mind and body. It reduces stress and it just feels good to get away from the hustle and bustle of life. If there's something on your mind then just distracting yourself for a short time throwing stones into the water sometimes makes the answer you've been looking for just pop into your consciousness.

Throw different shapes and weights of stones to see how they splash and make ripples in the water.

Skim a stone and see how many times it hits the water. The thinner and lighter stones are better and throw it, spinning it as low and as horizontal as you can.

I'm really proud of myself if I manage one skim but I better get practising if I want to beat the world record held by Russell Byars of 51 skims.

"Enjoy the little things, for one day you will look back and realise they were the big things."

- Robert Braul

Pooh Sticks

"Rivers know this: There is no hurry.
We shall get there some day."
- Winnie the Pooh

Pooh sticks was invented by A.A. Milne and first mentioned in "The house at Pooh Corner," a Winnie the Pooh book.

You play on a bridge over running water. Each person chooses a stick and drops it on the upstream side of the bridge at the same time. You then run to the other side of the bridge and the first stick that appears is the winner.

One piece of advice would be to make sure you all have similar size sticks or there will be all sorts of arguments if it is a close finish.

"You don't stop playing because you grow old; You grow old because you stop playing."

- George Bernard Shaw

Bake a cake

"Birthdays are nature's way of telling us to eat more cake."
- Author unknown

There is nothing nicer than the smell of a cake baking in the oven. It brings back memories of having to stand on a chair to reach the kitchen top, sticking fingers in the bowl to lick the left over batter and making figures out of the spare bits of pastry then baking them in the oven.

There are lots of recipes for cakes but I always end up making the same one. It's a simple Victorian sponge because even if it doesn't rise as much as it should or sometimes gets a bit burned around the edges I just simply cover it in icing and decorate with sweets and it's demolished by the family in seconds.

You only need:

100g (4oz) margarine, 100g (4oz) caster sugar, 100g (4oz) self-raising flour and 2 medium eggs.

Heat the oven to gas mark 4 or 180 C and grease an 18cm (7 inch) sandwich tin.

Cream the margarine and sugar until light and fluffy then beat in the eggs adding a little flour to stop it curdling. Fold in the remaining flour then pour in the tin and bake in the oven for about 40 minutes. It should be evenly brown and shrinking slightly away from the sides of the tin.

You could even cheat a little and use a box of cake mix. You'll still have the lovely aroma of a cake baking in the oven and you don't need to tell anyone it came from a box, that'll be our little secret.

"The world is more malleable than you think and it's waiting for you to hammer it into shape."

- Paul David Heuson

Icing biscuits

"Ever notice how 'what the hell' is always the right answer?"
- Marilyn Monroe

Buy a packet of digestive biscuits and make some icing or use the little tubes of coloured icing.

Cover the biscuit in the icing and decorate with sweets and sprinkles.

These are really yummy and you can make all sorts of patterns and funny faces with the decorations.

Having something naughty once in a while isn't going to do you any harm as long as you don't then spend the next couple of hours telling yourself how bad you've been. Remember the point is to have fun and enjoy!

When my youngest son was at primary school they would have a school fair every year to raise money. There would be stalls selling baked goods, second hand toys, vegetables grown from their garden, and lots more but one of the most popular stalls with the children was the one where they iced and decorated their own biscuit for a small amount of money.

So, if you're looking for any ideas for fundraising then give this one a go.

"Now and then it's good to pause in the pursuit of happiness and just be happy."

- Guillaume Apollinaire

Design your own pizza

"The only way to keep your health
is to eat what you don't want, drink what
you don't like and do what you'd rather not."
- Mark Twain

Buy some pizza bases, a jar of pizza sauce and a variety of your favourite toppings.

Put everything out on the kitchen table and let everyone choose what they want to put on their pizza, then bake in the oven.

This one is always a family favourite as everyone can make their own and choose their own toppings. If you can't eat a whole pizza then share a base with someone else and each decorates their own half.

Then when the pizzas come out of the oven be prepared for admiring glances and some "oohs and ahhs" and "I wish I'd put that on, it looks really good."

I've always found that if any of my children were bringing home friends who were fussy eaters for tea then letting them make their own pizza solved the problem of what to feed them.

Some people get very creative. My youngest son even made a pizza to represent a Mondrian painting for his art project at school, with the added benefit of eating it later.

"The more
we nourish
our internal
world, the more
powerful we grow
in the external
world."

- Susan L Taylor

Shrink crisp packets

"Curiouser and curiouser!"
Lewis Carroll, Alice in Wonderland

Use plastic (not foil) crisp packets.

Preheat oven to 250 degrees.

When you've eaten your crisps clean out the packet with a little soapy water

And dry.

Cover a baking tray with foil and place the crisp packet on the tray.

Put in the oven for 2 to 3 minutes.

Carefully take the tray out and you should have a tiny crisp packet.

If you're making a key ring or badge with it then punch the holes in the packet before you bake it.

"Doctor, Doctor, I think I'm shrinking."

"Well, take these tablets but you'll have to be a little patient."

"If you cannot do great things, do small things in a great way."

- Napoleon Hill

Bed-time story

"That's the real trouble with the world,
too many people grow up."
- Walt Disney

Draw the curtains, put on the bedside lamp and get all cosy and comfortable in your bed

Get your partner to read to you and for a bit of fun they could make up voices for the different characters. Do you remember when your mum or dad would make a big, deep voice for the big daddy bear and a small squeaky voice for the baby bear?

Ask your children to read to you for a change or tell them it's practice for their homework to read to you, they will like 'being in charge' of the story telling.

Listen to a story on the radio or get a CD of someone reading a book you've always wanted to read but never had the time to. The chances are you'll fall asleep after the first few chapters which makes this a particularly good way to get off to sleep if you need to take your mind off work or something that's bothering you.

"We tend to forget that happiness doesn't come as a result of getting something we don't have, but rather of recognising and appreciating what we do have."

- Frederick Keonig

Read a fairy tale

"If I'm honest I have to tell you, I still read
fairy tales and I like them best of all."
- Audrey Hepburn

We all know the Disney versions of Rapunzel, Cinderella, little red riding hood etc, but how many of us have read the original stories by the Brothers Grimm.

The tales are often dark and cruel, and there's not always a happy ending. Sometimes there's a moral to the story, a lesson to be learned.

There's a part of us that likes to lose ourselves in a magical story about handsome princes fighting dragons for the hand of the beautiful princess and the wicked stepmother getting her comeuppance.

Enjoy the magic of fairytales and being lost in your imagination for a little while.

On long, dark winter nights people would sit around the fire listening to folktales, myths and legends being told. Recreate the atmosphere by reading a story by candlelight to your family. The flickering of the candlelight in the darkness and the silence while you read aloud with everyone hanging on to your words makes for a special, close family moment.

"In dreams and in love there are no impossibilities."

- Janos Aray

Go out in the rain

"Anyone who says sunshine brings happiness has never
danced in the rain."
- Author unknown

The next time its raining go outside and get absolutely soaking
wet. Jump in the puddles, splash about in the puddles, stick your
tongue out and your hands out and try and catch the rain. Just
let yourself go have some fun and be glad to be alive.

If you're a bit more of the quiet type and don't like to draw
attention to yourself then just leave the umbrella at home keep
your hood down and simply look up to the sky and feel the rain
on your face.

One of my most romantic memories is when my husband and I
were on a summer holiday in Lake Garda, Italy. We were going
back to our hotel one evening when it started to pour with
rain but really lovely warm rain. Laughing and running through
the foreign streets getting absolutely drenched and soaked right
through was one of those wonderful moments Phil and I will
never forget.

"Each of us
makes his own
weather,
determines
the colour of
the skies
in the emotional
universe which he
inhabits."

- Fulton J Sheen

Scare yourself

"Look out it's behind you!"

Do you remember as a child being too scared to go past a certain house because you were told a witch lived there? Hearing strange noises in the night and thinking that a monster was hiding under your bed ready to grab your leg as you walked past.

Did the big boys and girls scare you with stories of someone being bitten by a spider and having lots of baby spiders hatching in their body?

I dare you, sit in the dark and watch a scary film. You can hide behind a cushion if that will make you feel better

Go on one of the many tours you find in most cities that take you around haunted sites and tell you stories of witches and ghosts. Whoooooooooo!

Read a horror classic like Dracula or Frankenstein.

Get out of your comfort zone and do at least one thing that scares you on a regular basis.

Fear and excitement can have the same physical sensations, feeling sick, nervous tummy, the shakes. Instead of thinking you're feeling scared try and change your thought to one of feeling excitement and anticipation. It might be the difference between an exciting new experience and missing out on a great opportunity.

"Do one thing every day that scares you."

- Eleanor Roosevelt

Play hide and seek in the dark

"Just play. Have fun. Enjoy the game."
- Michael Jordan

This is a great game to play when the nights are drawing in and it gets dark early. If you're a bit of a scaredy cat you could use a torch but it does make it easier to find people.

When I was a child my sister and I used to play hide and seek in the dark with our dad in our small two bedroom flat. My dad was an expert hider and one of his favourite places was in the wardrobe where he'd move the coats about to hide himself.

When we found him we would carefully reach out to touch him and say "got you!" but he wouldn't move or speak so we'd say it again but he still wouldn't do anything and because it was so dark we couldn't see him. Then all of a sudden he would jump out and chase us around the flat. It was terrifying but we always wanted to play it again and again!

"I learned that courage was not the absence of fear, but the triumph over it. The brave man is not he who does not feel afraid, but he who conquers that fear."

- Nelson Mandela

Play cards

"If you must play, decide on three things at the start: the
rules of the game, the stakes, and the quitting time"
- Chinese proverb

Do you remember the card games you used to play with your
friends? Snap, old maid, 21, happy families, concentration.

It's sometimes easy to forget in this electronic age the simple
pleasure of sitting round the table with family and friends playing
cards.

Why not organise a games night once a month. Get some drinks
and treats, switch the telly off, have a stack of spare change handy
and enjoy spending time together.

Have a competition to see who can build the tallest card pyramid,
just don't get annoyed if someone knocks it down.

A man walked by a table in a hotel and noticed 3 men and a dog
playing cards. The dog was playing with great skill. "This is a
very smart dog," the man commented.

"Not so smart", said one of the players, "Every time he gets a
good hand he wags his tail."

- Unknown

"Each player must accept the cards life deals him or her, but once they are in hand, he or she alone must decide how to play the cards in order to win the game."

- Voltaire

Play a board game

"Life is more fun if you play games."
- Roald Dahl, *My Uncle Oswald*

How many of us have boxes of board games hidden away in garages and lofts that we only seem to bring out at Christmas. I don't know if it's because the rules can be too complicated, they take too long to set up or the games seem to go on forever. Then when we do decide to play them we open the box only to find pieces missing.

Yet there's something about getting the family together and playing the old favourites; Monopoly, Cluedo, Risk, Mousetrap and arguing about who is going to have what piece, arguing about who won the last time, arguing about who should go first, arguing about who cheated. OOPS! I think I realise why we don't play board games that often.

But if you get a game that everyone enjoys then how does it get any better than that, spending quality time with each other, laughing, having fun and making happy memories.

So, don't just wait until Christmas, get everyone together and play some board games.

"It's the game of life. Do I win or do I lose? One day they're gonna shut the game down. I gotta have as much fun and go around the board as many times as I can before it's my turn to leave."

- Tupac Shakur

Watch Cartoons

"I have the power."
- He Man

You could always tell it was the school holidays because all the cartoons were on the telly through the week. There was nothing better than sitting in your pyjamas, eating your cornflakes knowing there was no rush to get ready while watching Tom and Jerry or Scooby Doo.

Why not this Saturday go downstairs in your pyjamas get a bowl of coco pops or whatever you enjoyed for breakfast as a child and sit on the couch and watch your favourite cartoons. You can get them on DVD or some of the children's channels replay the ones we used to enjoy.

Have a look at the cartoons children watch now and you may find yourself with some new favourites like Sponge Bob Squarepants.

Last Valentine's Day my husband brought home Disney's Beauty and the Beast. I love that film and I had wanted it on DVD for ages. We had a lovely evening watching the film, drinking wine and eating chocolates.

"Don't take life too seriously; you'll never get out alive."

- Bugs Bunny

Make a vision board

"Happiness lies in the joy of achievement
and the thrill of creative effort."
- Franklin D. Roosevelt

Creating a vision board is a powerful way to visualise your goals and make things happen in your life. It keeps you focused on goals and dreams.

Decide what you want in your life; healthy body, the ideal partner, holiday of a lifetime, the perfect house......

Cut out images, words and phrases that inspire you from old magazines, brochures, catalogues and stick them on a cork board with pins or glue. Jazz it up a bit by adding glitter, stickers and ribbons.

Make sure you look at your board every day.

We made a family holiday vision board for a holiday in America. We got brochures from the travel agents and cut out pictures of the places we'd like to visit and things we wanted to do which included renewing our wedding vows by Elvis in Las Vegas. The board was put on the wall in the kitchen along with our individual vision boards so we would see them every time we went into the kitchen and because they looked so bright and colourful.

It worked for us....... Viva Las Vegas!

"You are never too old to set another goal or to dream a new dream."

- C.S. Lewis

Dance

"Those who were seen dancing were thought to be
insane by those who could not hear the music."
-Friedrick Nietzsche

Put on your favourite music, play it loud, kick off your shoes and
dance your heart out. Shake your booty, wave your hands in the
air, and swing your hair around. Move to the rhythm of the music
around your living room.

Join that dance or exercise class it'll keep you fit, help you meet
new people and is fun to do.

If you're too shy then buy the DVD and practice at home.

Check out any clubs that play your kind of music and go dancing
with friends.

Go on! What are you waiting for?

I managed to persuade my husband to try a salsa class and
eventually he agreed, (probably because it was being held in a
pub). We had a good laugh learning the basic moves and trying to
keep in time with the music. We didn't even consider it as doing
exercise until in the morning we woke up with aching muscles.

"Dance as if no-one's watching, sing as if no-one's listening and live every day as if it were your last."

- Irish proverb

Doodle

"Mickey Mouse popped out of my mind onto a drawing
pad 20 years ago on a train ride from Manhattan
to Hollywood at a time when business fortunes
of my brother Roy and myself were at lowest ebb
and disaster seemed right around the corner."
-Walt Disney

Do you remember sitting at your desk in the classroom half listening to the teacher as you scribbled a border around the page of your school book? Writing with felt tip pens the names of your favourite bands over and over. Drawing flowers, cute animals and love hearts with you and the person you fancied initials in the centre.

Doodles are what we produce in our idle moments when the focus of our attention is elsewhere, we're bored or stressed.

Doodles can be very revealing about our personality because we doodle without thinking.

Far from not paying attention research has shown that doodling helps retain information and that doodlers actually have better recall than those just sitting listening.

So get doodling. Just draw whatever comes into your head. If you can't think of anything, then start with an animal, flower or face and see what comes from there. You could also write down a word like happy or rich then draw what you associate with these things. Use felt tips or coloured pencils to add a splash of colour if you want.

"Everything you can imagine is real."

- Pablo Picasso

Join a club

"I refuse to join any club that would have me as a member."
- Groucho Marx

How many of us were in the brownies, guides, scouts, or a member of a judo, football, drama club held in the local church hall and community centre.

Chances are that most of us have tried at least one club in our childhood even if we only went for the first few weeks.

Joining a club is a good way to make friends, participate in an activity you enjoy, develop skills and extend your knowledge. Even in the smallest of communities there's always some kind of club from crafts and arts to local history and rambling.

If there's not, then why don't you start your own? Ask around your friends and neighbours to see if they're interested. You could discuss books, play cards, knit. It could be a different thing each week and you could take it in turns to hold it at each other's homes.

A friend invited me to the badminton club at our sports centre, so I went along with my only experience being of playing badminton in the garden with the kids. Some of the people there had obviously been playing a long time and knew what they were doing but there were also others like me who were new to it all. But you know what, it didn't matter. I was meeting new people, I was learning, I was getting exercise and more importantly – it was fun.

"Promise me you'll always remember: You're braver than you believe, and *stronger* than you *seem*, and smarter than you think."

- A.A. Milne

Jump on a trampoline

"A bear, however hard he tries, grows tubby without exercise."
- AA Milne, Winnie the Pooh

Jumping up and down on a trampoline stimulates lymphatic drainage so is detoxifying and some women say it has reduced their cellulite. It's easy on the joints, burns loads of calories and it's a fun way to exercise.

Get yourself a mini trampoline to jump on while you're watching the TV.

Six minutes on the trampoline can be the equivalent of a one mile jog.

If the kids have a trampoline in the garden why not give it a go. Jump as high as you can, it feels like flying, bounce onto your bum and if you're feeling brave do a front flip.

When I was younger my friends and I would take great delight in jumping up and down on the bed singing the song "5 little monkeys jumping on the bed" then taking it in turns to fall out while the others wagged their finger and sang, "and the doctor said, no more monkeys jumping on the bed!"

"The great man is he who does not lose his childlike heart."

- Mencius

Make a funny face

"Mirror, mirror here I stand. Who is the fairest in the land?"
- Grimm's fairytales

Screw up your face, pout, puff out your cheeks, and suck in your cheeks. Stick out your tongue, try and touch your nose with your tongue. Make as many funny faces as you can and if anyone should see you just tell them you're doing facial exercises to tone up and smooth out your face.

Every time you look in the mirror stick your tongue out at yourself

Now, I know as we get older looking in the mirror is not always a comfortable thing to do. As Bette Davis said, "old age ain't no place for sissies." Instead of criticizing yourself, that's just too easy, be kinder to yourself and look for something to appreciate and affirm regularly,

"I am amazing at every age."

"I have looked in the mirror every morning and asked myself:

'If today were the last day of my life, would I want to do what I am about to do today?'

And whenever the answer has been 'NO' for too many days in a row, I know I need to change something."

- Steve Jobs

Go on an adventure

"When you see someone putting on his big boots, you
can be pretty sure an adventure is going to happen."
- Winnie the Pooh

If you look back through your life there's probably been lots of
things that you have been nervous and scared about doing, riding
your bike without stabilisers, your first day at school, learning to
swim without armbands. When you faced your fear and did it you
felt great, you had a sense of empowerment and wondered why
you had been so scared to do it in the first place.

Go for it! I dare you! Do that thing you've always wanted to do.

If it seems too big then break it down into smaller steps. Do
research, speak to people, start a savings account.

How does it feel when you imagine yourself doing it? Are you
excited, scared, exhilarated all at the same time?

Once you want something you can't go back to not wanting it.
It's always there in the back of your mind and keeps popping up
throughout your life reminding you that there is something you
want to do or be.

Life is too short for regrets!

"Whatever you can do, or dream you can do, begin it. Boldness has genius, power, and magic in it. Begin it now."

- Johan Wolfgang von Goethe

Do a headstand

"It's kind of fun to do the impossible."
- Walt Disney

Doing a headstand can be scary, it really does turn your world upside down but according to yoga philosophy time spent upside down every day is one of the best things you can do for yourself.

Not only will it build your confidence up because "I did it, yeah!" but there are many health benefits including:

It gives your heart a rest by allowing gravity to direct blood to your brain which increases your mental power and concentration.

More nutrients and oxygen are flowing to your face giving you a mini facelift and a glow to your skin.

Delays the onset of grey hair and is even supposed to reverse grey hair back to its natural colour (I live in hope).

Doing a headstand also tones the abdomen, legs and neck muscles.

If you're feeling brave try a handstand.

Just be careful and maybe do it against a wall until you've got more confidence.

"The purpose of life is to live it, to take experience to the utmost, to reach out eagerly and without fear for newer and richer experience."

- Eleanor Roosevelt

Do a roly-poly

"I used to want the words 'She tried' on my
tombstone. Now I want 'she did it.'"
- Katherine Dunham

Wear clothes that you don't mind getting grass stains or a bit of dirt on.

Check the hill or grassy slope you're going to roll down is free from any sticks, stones or nasty surprises!

Stand at the top and lie down horizontally, keep your arms tucked in then roll sideways down the hill. Roll over and over until you get to the bottom and let the world whizz by.

Don't sit up straight away as you may feel a wee bit dizzy! Then get up and do it again (and again) just for fun!

Another childhood song and game I also liked to play was "there were 5 in the bed." My friends and I would lie in bed and sing "there were 5 in the bed and the little one said, roll over, roll over so they all rolled over and one fell out" (which we would do) then we would continue "there were 4 in the bed." Until "there was one in the bed and the little one said goodnight."

"Our business is
to be happy"

- Dalai Lama

Move your body

"I said to the gym instructor – "Can you teach
me to do the splits?" He said "How flexible are
you?" I said, "I can't make Tuesdays.""
- Tommy Cooper

Remember as a child how you would twist your body into all
sorts of positions. Maybe you could do the splits or the crab. Did
you try and put your leg behind your neck?

How does your body feel now? Does it feel stiff? Do you have
aches and pains? Can you bend over without groaning and
touching your back?

The good news is, it's never too late to get your body moving
in ways that you haven't moved it for years, and one of the best
ways is to join a yoga class.

A yoga class is a safe and fun way to get your body moving.
Even if it's something that's never appealed to you before just
give it a go. It's a safe and effective way to increase strength and
flexibility. There's also evidence that regular yoga practice is
beneficial for people with depression and stress.

Please don't think these classes are full of young skinnies getting
into all sorts of strange positions. A typical class has a mix of
people of all ages, abilities and body types. Also everyone is so
busy concentrating on their own moves that nobody is going to
be looking or judging what you're doing.

"There are only two mistakes one can make along the road to truth; not going all the way and not starting."

- Buddha

Skip around the house

"Inside every old person is a young person
wondering what happened."
- Terry Pratchett

Give it a go! Skip from room to room. Swing your arms as you skip along.

It will lift your mood, make you feel lighter, happier, and more playful making anyone that sees you smile.

If you're not bothered about what people think then go outside and skip down the street. If you are bothered, check first that no one's looking then go for it and if someone should see you I bet they're thinking they wish they were brave enough to do that because it looks like so much fun.

My youngest son saw me skipping around the house one day and just rolled his eyes and shook his head so I told him not to knock it until he'd tried it.

A few days later I saw him skipping out of the kitchen. "What do you think?" I asked. "It felt good" he said.

"You were born
with wings.
Why prefer to
crawl through
life?"

- Rumi

Chalk on the pavement

"All real works of art look as though they were done in joy."
- Robert Henri

Buy some chalks and let your inner artist out by drawing on the pavement. Don't get too precious about your art work though because the rain will soon wash it off.

Play hide and seek outside where the people hiding draw chalk arrows on the ground as they go from place to place and the lookers have to find the arrows and follow them.

Do you remember playing hopscotch as a child and using a stone to mark out the squares when you didn't have any chalk.

How to Play Hopscotch: Chalk a hopscotch design on the pavement. The two basic rules to remember are that you can only have 1 foot in each square and remember to hop over the square with the rock in it.

First player throws their rock onto the first square. They then hop over that square to the second square on one foot. On double squares you must land with your feet side by side. Turn around and come back the same way only when you get to the square with your rock you must balance on one foot and pick up your rock. If completed with no mistakes then the player goes again and throws their rock to the 2 square and so on. If while throwing the rock you miss the right square or it lands on a line then you lose your turn. You also lose your turn if you step on a line, miss a square or lose your balance.

"Don't be afraid to take a big step when one is indicated. You can't cross a chasm in two small steps."

- David Lloyd George

Hop

"Whenever I feel the need to exercise,
I lie down until it goes away."
- Paul Terry

Hop on one leg and count how many hops you can manage then see if you can get the same or more on the other leg. It's probably better for you to set a time limit of maybe a minute for the first time as you can really feel the muscles working in your leg and bum.

Instead of walking from room to room try hopping, it'll get your heart rate up and help burn off those calories.

Ladies make sure you've got a good bra on!

Get yourself a space hopper. Remember that big, rubber, orange ball with horns to hold onto and make exercising fun. If you can get a friend to join you then have a race. If you've got the space make an obstacle course to go around. Who says you can't have a giggle working out?

"People rarely succeed unless they have fun in what they are doing."

- Dale Carnegie

Skipping rope

"Energy and persistence conquer all things."
- Benjamin Franklin

Get a skipping rope and see if you can do all your old tricks, criss-cross, skipping backward and bumps.

Do you remember the songs you used to sing while skipping? "I like coffee; I like tea, sausages in the pan........."

Try and get family and friends involved and take turns jumping in and doing the actions.

If you need any more encouragement to pick up a skipping rope or old washing line then how about the health benefits that skipping brings such as being easier on your joints than running, (ten minutes of skipping can have the same health benefits as a 45 minute run).

It's a full body workout that you can do at your own pace improving heart rate, blood pressure, stamina. In fact there's a list as long as my arm about all the benefits. Just give it a go and see for yourself.

"The most important thing is to enjoy your life—to be happy—it's all that matters."

- Audrey Hepburn

Jump over the cracks in the pavement

"I need only one superstition. I made sure to touch all the bases when I hit a home run."
- Babe Ruth

What superstitions did you have as a child? Maybe you still have them?

-   Cross your fingers for good luck or when you tell a lie.
-   Don't walk under a ladder
-   If you break a mirror you'll have 7 years bad luck.
-   Having an itchy ear means someone is talking about you.
-   Knock on wood so you don't jinks yourself
-   Find a penny pick it up, all day long you'll have good luck.

It's quite common in top athletes to have a specific ritual they follow before an event such as listening to certain music, eating a particular food or wearing a particular shirt or underwear.

They believe it makes them perform better and gets them into the winning zone.

The tennis player Bjorn Borg would grow out his beard for Wimbledon and footballer David Beckham wore a new pair of boots for every game.

Go on be honest; do you have a lucky pair of pants?

"Put your heart, mind and soul into even your smallest acts. This is the secret of success."

- Swami Sivanand

Get someone to play with your hair

"Forget not that the earth delights to feel your bare
feet and the winds long to play with your hair."
- Khalil Gibran

There are many reasons why having your hair played with feels
sooooo good! It helps to relax and calm us, it feels lovely and
tingly, add in a scalp massage and you'll be in seventh heaven.

See if you can get your partner to play with your hair with the
promise you'll return the favour.

Or ask one of your children.

If you've never had an Indian head massage then treat yourself.
You'll never want it to end. Pure bliss! Make sure you go straight
home after as they put oil on your hair to help condition it.

I used to love playing hairdressers with my children when they
were younger and I used to pretend to go to their salon and get
my hair done. When it was over I might have looked like I had
been dragged through a hedge backwards but it was worth it.

"Follow your bliss and the universe will open doors for you where there were only walls."

- Joseph Campbell

Fly a kite

"Those who fly a kite can have a long life."
- Chinese saying

Being outdoors and being at one with nature. Feeling the wind in your face and looking at the beauty of the sky. Breathing in the fresh air and exercising your body; you can see why flying a kite is good for you as well as being a fun activity to do by yourself or with others.

There are various types of kites depending on how serious you are. We picked up a cheap one from a toy store but if you're feeling creative make and decorate your own kite. Do you remember cutting out a diamond shape from paper and sticking straws or sticks on to form a T shape, then decorating the kite with bold colours and gluing on a crepe paper streamer and bows. Or did you simply tie a plastic carrier bag to some string.

When you fly the kite it's better to have someone to help you. They can hold the kite while you pull the string out.

Just be careful if like us you have a mad dog who thinks the kite is his new toy and it's fun to run away with it in his mouth while we chase after him.

"Childhood is measured out by sounds and smells and sights, before the dark hour of reason grows."

- John Betjeman

Pretend

"There is no life I know to compare
with pure imagination. Living there you'll be
free if you truly wish to be."
- Roald Dahl

Did you want to be a princess or a cowboy when you were a child? Did you pretend the cardboard box was a spaceship or castle?

Who says you have to stop pretending when you grow up? Have some fun and....

Go into that shop and try on the expensive dress or suit, imagine going to the ball or awards ceremony.

Visit the car showroom and sit in the car that you've dreamed of owning. Smell the leather, feel the dashboard. Imagine yourself driving the car through the streets or better still go on a test drive.

Spend an afternoon browsing round shops looking for furniture, carpets, curtains, everything you would want to put into your fantasy home Anything that takes your fancy, say to yourself "That's for me, I can have that, I could have that in every colour if I wanted to. I can afford that, and that."

Daydream about being a famous actor, author or pop star.

Pretend and have some fun with it. It feels good and who knows what could come from it.

"There is nothing like a dream to create the future."

- Victor Hugo

Sing

"Doc I can't stop singing, The Green, Green
Grass of Home." "That sounds like Tom Jones
syndrome." 'Is it common?' "It's not unusual.'"
- Tommy Cooper

Singing is good for your health. When you sing your body
produces feel good endorphins making you feel happy and
uplifted. You're exercising your heart, lungs and muscle groups
in the upper body.

Join a choir and make new friends. There's even research that
shows this may help you live longer as it promotes a healthy heart
and an enhanced mental state.

Learn the words to your favourite song and sing it loudly, just let
yourself go and feel how good it is to sing at the top of your voice.

Go with a group of friends to a pub with a karaoke machine and
laugh at each other's singing, or be impressed by their talent.

Sing in the car and don't be put off by your children's comments.

Get some singing lessons. (That's just a suggestion, not an
observation.)

My husband was never interested in getting a karaoke machine
but one Christmas we got "Sing Star" for the X box. He's now
the first one on and the last one off. Usually he's left with the
dog, who seems to be the only one in the family who appreciates
his singing.

"A bird does not sing because it has an answer. It sings because it has a song."

- Chinese proverb

Play a musical instrument

"I'm playing all the right notes—but not
necessarily in the right order."
- Morecambe and Wise

Wanting to be able to play a musical instrument is a desire that
a lot of us have but it just seems like too much effort and hard
work. Yet with practice and discipline it is possible, and that
sense of achievement when you manage to play your first piece
is unforgettable

Learning something that is new and challenging is also a good
way to keep your mind active and alert. A study by St Andrews
University showed that playing an instrument could sharpen
the mind. Their results indicated musical activity could be used
to slow, stop or even reverse age and illness-related decline in
mental functioning.

If that still sounds like too much work then just have some fun.
Get yourself a tambourine or maracas and make some noise!

"Music gives a soul to the universe, wings to the mind, flight to the imagination and life to everything."

- Plato

Be naughty

"When I'm good, I'm very good,
but when I'm bad, I'm better."
- Mae West

Do you remember?

- Playing knocky-nine-doors, when you'd ring someone's door bell and run away.
- Making prank phone calls.
- Playing football beside the "no ball games" sign.
- Skipping school.
- Trying to get into somewhere without paying.
- Getting into a film when you were underage.
- Not coming home on time.

I dare you!

The next time you're in a lift, press all the buttons before you get out.

Give your partner a dirty phone call at work.

Get a tattoo.

Buy those expensive shoes you've always wanted.

Have a night out through the week even if you have work the next day.

The next time you say to yourself "should I, or shouldn't I?" You should.

Play strip poker.

When it was our wedding anniversary, Phil and I went away for the weekend. We were going to go to the cinema, shopping etc. On our first day we had a nice lunch at a bar that sold cocktails. There were a few we hadn't tried before, so we had one, then another and before we knew it, we ended up in a tattoo parlour getting matching tattoos.

"To live is the rarest thing in the world.
Most people exist, that is all."

- Oscar Wilde

Go to the seaside

"I'd give all the wealth that years have piled,
the slow result of life's decay, to be once
more a little child for one bright summer day."
- Lewis Carroll

Our homes and workplaces generate an abundance of positive ions from computers, fluorescent lighting, heating systems and televisions that can make us feel tired and irritable. Sea air is charged with healthy negative ions which strengthen the immune system, improve our mood and help us to sleep better.

Get your bucket and spade and take a trip to the seaside!

Spend a day at the seaside and breathe in that lovely, fresh sea air.
Go paddling in the sea and jump over the waves.
Look for pretty shells and pebbles.
Write messages in the sand.
Build a sandcastle with a moat and fill it up with buckets of seawater.
Stay until the tide comes in and covers your sandcastle
Watch the sunset.
Close your eyes and just listen to the sound of the waves.
Get a big portion of fish and chips and feed the left-overs to seagulls.

If you can't make it to the seaside buy yourself a CD that plays the sound of waves on the seashore. The calming, relaxing quality of the ocean sounds helps clear the mind and aid relaxation.

"Live in the sunshine, swim in the sea, drink the wild air."

- Ralph Waldo Emerson

Go for a bike ride

"When the spirits are low, when the day appears dark, when work becomes monotonous, when hope hardly seems worth having, just mount a bicycle and go out for a spin down the road, without thought on anything but the ride you are taking."
- Sir Arthur Conan Doyle

Get your bike out the garage, hire or borrow one.

Cycle around streets and places you only ever pass in your car. You'll notice things that you've never seen before even though you may have driven that way every day.

Cycle to a pub in the country and have a nice lunch then cycle back and burn off the calories.

Leave the car at home and cycle to work. You'll improve your fitness, lose weight and be helping the environment.

Spend quality time with the family and take a picnic with you.

Fly down a hill with your feet off the pedals.

Even just cycling around your local park enjoying the scenery is a pleasant way to spend some time in the fresh air and great exercise.

It doesn't matter if you've not ridden a bike for years because it's one of those things you never forget to do. You may be a bit wobbly at first but it's just like........

"Life is like riding a bicycle. To keep your balance, you must keep moving."

- Albert Einstein

Give yourself pocket money

"All I ask is the chance to prove that
money can't make me happy."
- Spike Milligan

I don't know what the going rate is for pocket money but why not give yourself a set amount of money each week and treat yourself.

Buy a magazine, CD, big box of chocolates, go for coffee and cake.

I know that a lot of people can buy these things without giving it a second thought but there is still something special about having your own pocket money. It's like at Christmas or your birthday and someone gives you a gift card. It's a nice feeling thinking about what you're going to spend it on.

You've worked hard for it and you deserve it!

I remember going to the newsagents on a Saturday morning with my pocket money to buy the comic "Twinkle" and some sweets. Then spend the rest of the morning reading about "Nurse Nancy" and cutting out the cut-out doll and dresses.

My oldest son would always spend his pocket money on Pokémon stickers or football stickers that he put in a book. I will always remember his happiness when it was the sticker he needed to complete the team and the disappointment when it was a doubler (or swapsie), and all for only a few pence!

"There are people who have money and people who are rich."

- Coco Chanel

Piggy bank

"A man walks into a bar looking sad. The barman
says, 'You look like you need a drink.' The man
replies, 'That's the problem – I can't drink with
what I've got.' Concerned the barman asks 'Oh no!
What have you got?' The man replies '10p'"

Instead of all those small coins taking up space in your purse
stick them in a piggy bank and you'll be amazed at how quickly
it adds up to a more substantial amount.

Pick the piggy bank up on a regular basis to give it a shake and
feel how heavy it's getting.

You don't even need to count it up into money bags to take to the
bank as most supermarkets have machines that you tip your coins
into and for a small charge will give you a voucher to exchange
for the cash in the supermarket.

How many times did you open your piggy bank when you were
younger to find an IOU note from your mum or dad saying they
had borrowed some money from your bank?

My son got a swear box that every time you put money into it,
bleeps and whistles. He makes a small fortune out of it during
the football season thanks to his dad.

"Fortune sides
with him who
dares."

- Virgil

Go on a picnic

"Where should I go?" – Alice
"That depends on where you want to
end up." – The Cheshire Cat
- Lewis Carroll, Alice in Wonderland

You can make it as simple as some sandwiches, sausage rolls and crisps with bottles of juice and a flask of tea in a carrier bag, to food prepared by the local deli and bottles of champagne in a wicker picnic basket with china plates and cutlery.

Gather together a group of family and friends take bats and balls, cricket set and a football. Play games, share food and create fun, happy memories.

Don't forget a rug to sit on.

And if it rains just sit in the car nice and dry, listening to the rain hitting the windows enjoying your sandwiches.

"Adopt the pace of nature: her secret is patience."

- Ralph Waldo Emerson

Have a tea party

"If this is coffee, please bring me some tea, but
if this is tea, please bring me some coffee."
- Abraham Lincoln

Make it special by sending out invitations either homemade or shop bought.

Get out the teapot, cups and saucers, milk and sugar jugs that are normally hidden away in the back of the cupboard.

Buy or make sandwiches and cakes then cut them into small, dainty pieces.

Set the table with a tablecloth and vase of flowers. If there are children fill a teapot with juice.

For grown-ups who want something stronger make some cocktails and serve in a teapot and teacup.

Or you could get someone else to do all the work and go out to a hotel for afternoon tea with some friends.

My daughter and I sometimes meet up with my mum, sister and niece and go for afternoon tea to a posh hotel for a girls day out. It's a great way to catch up in lovely surroundings and eat cake.

"May you live
every day of your
life."

- Jonathan Swift

Paint a picture

"If you hear a voice within you say
'You cannot paint', then by all means paint
and that voice will be silenced."
- Vincent Van Gogh

If you've always wanted to paint but think you can't then here's some advice from two old masters.

"When you go out and paint, try and forget what you have before you – a tree, a house, a field or whatever. Merely think here is a little square of blue, here an oblong of pink, here a streak of yellow, and paint it just as it looks to you, the exact colour and shape, until it emerges as your own naive impression of the scene before you."
- Claude Monet

You could always cheat a little and use a painting by numbers kit.

Join an art club to meet people, learn something new, socialise and have fun.

Painting takes you to your own space away from everyday reality, lowering your stress levels and relaxing you. When you immerse yourself totally in what you're doing time passes by without you noticing.

Be proud of what you've created and display them on your walls. You never know, you might have a talent that could bring in an income.

"This world is but a canvas to our imagination."

- Henry David Thoreau

Colouring-in

"Artists are just children who refuse
to put down their crayons."
- Al Hirschfeld

If you're feeling a bit stressed out then simply spending some quiet time colouring-in can really calm you down and get your thoughts together. Try it and see.

It's also something to do on those long flight or train journeys to pass some time when you've read all your magazines.

Don't just use the kids colouring-in books, choose your own one and get some crayons, coloured pencils or felt tip pens that are just for you and buy a pencil case to keep them in.

If you're particularly proud of any of your colouring-ins then frame them and put on the wall.

"Life is really simple, but we insist on making it complicated."

- Confucius

Play Kissy Catch

"No, I don't think I will kiss you, although you need
kissing, badly. That's what's wrong with you. You should
be kissed and often, and by someone who knows how."
- Margaret Mitchell, *Gone with the Wind*

I don't know which is more fun doing the chasing or being
chased. Go on, I dare you, chase each other round the house and
give a big, sloppy kiss!

Did you know, Philematology is the study of kissing?

Kissing someone we care for lowers stress levels and makes us
happy. It strengthens our relationships and is even supposed
to make us healthier. The exchange of saliva stimulates your
immune system to produce antibodies which helps your body
fight infection. You only have to think of when you were a child
and grazed your knee and went crying to your parents to get it
kissed better.

A gentle, loving kiss makes everything seem better and not only
that but it burns calories too. Not many, but hey who's counting?

Even getting into the habit of giving your partner a kiss before
you leave in the morning and when you get home at night keeps
the intimacy alive in your relationship and shows how much you
care for each other.

"Being happy doesn't mean that everything is perfect. It means that you've decided to look beyond the imperfections."

- Anonymous

Have a (fun) fight

"I am the greatest; I said that even before I knew I was."
- Muhammad Ali

Train your mind and strengthen your body as well as learning self-defence by joining a martial arts or boxing class.

Have a pillow fight but make sure you don't hit each other too hard as it may be a soft pillow but it can still hurt.

Play a computer game and beat up your opponents.

If there's enough of you play British Bulldogs. One person is the bulldog and they stand in the middle of the play area with everyone else standing in line at the end. When the one in the middle shouts "BULLDOG" everyone has to try and run to the other end without being caught by the bulldog. If you are caught then you have to join the bulldog. The winner is the last player not caught.

My youngest son who's 11, husband and I joined a tae kwon do class to try and get Liam to do something other than play on his X box all day.

The good thing about these classes is the mix of age and abilities. It's a great way of doing exercise without becoming bored, it's fun and something we can share as a family.

And what better way to release some tension than by punching and kicking the pads, especially if your husband's holding them.

"That's for not doing............." (Kick)
"Take that for............" (Punch)
All I can say is you'll feel so much better afterwards.

"If you always put limits on everything you do, physical or anything else, it will spread into your work and into your life. There are no limits. There are only plateaus, and you must not stay there, you must go beyond them."

- Bruce Lee

Have a nap

"I have left orders to be awakened at any
time during national emergency, even if I'm
in a cabinet meeting."
- Ronald Reagan

A short nap of 20 minutes may help you feel better and give you more energy to carry on with your day.

History is full of famous people who enjoyed a nap – Napoleon, Winston Churchill, John F Kennedy to name just a few.

If Thomas Edison was seeking solutions he would take a nap and receive the insights he needed in his sleep.

So, the next time you need an answer to anything why don't you try having a nap and see if your sub-conscious will come up with any suggestions,

Then write down straight away anything that comes up.

There's also something that feels quite naughty about going to bed in the afternoon for a little snooze.

"All men dream but not all equally. Those who dream by night, in the dusty recesses of their minds, wake to find it was all vanity. But the dreamers of the day are dangerous, for they may act their dreams with open eyes and make things happen."

- T E Lawrence

Cover yourself in mud

> "A little nonsense now and then is
> cherished by the wisest men."
> - Roald Dahl, *Charlie and the great glass elevator*

As well as making your skin feel lovely and soft, mud has many health benefits and has been used for thousands of years

Buy or make some body mud and cover yourself from head to toe in mud. Better still take it in turns with your partner to cover each other in mud. To try and reduce the mess do it in the shower then you can hose each other down afterwards.

Have a mud bath. There are plenty of beauty products out there that you can add to your bath and don't let the colour of the water put you off.

Put a mud face pack on.

If the thought of all that mess is too much then treat yourself to a visit to a spa and let them do all the work.

I went to a spa for a mud wrap for the first time not knowing what to expect. When the therapist has covered you with mud they bind you so tight you can't move your arms and legs then the therapist leaves you for 20 minutes. I had to get her to leave the door open a little and keep checking in on me because I hated that feeling of being trapped. And of course as soon as you can't move your arms, your nose starts itching.

"Always laugh
when you can,
it is cheap
medicine."

- Lord Byron

Buy a pick and mix

"Families are like fudge, mostly sweet with a few nuts."
- Unknown

There's something that takes you right back to your childhood when you're faced with rows and rows of sweets. The pressure of choosing the right sweets out of all that choice especially when you only had a few pence to spend and you were getting hurried up by your mum or the shopkeeper. You wanted the cola cubes and some penny chews but you also liked the black jacks..... oooh decisions!

Get one of the tubs and fill it up with all those sweets you like and some you've never tried. Take your time and fill it to the brim.

Don't eat them all at once or you'll get a sore tummy!

If you're being really good then just have one or two of your favourites and take them into the office to share around.

"There is only one way to avoid criticism: do nothing, say nothing, and be nothing."

— Aristotle

Go to the ice-cream van

"Age does not diminish the extreme disappointment
of having a scoop of ice cream fall from the cone."
-Jim Fiebig

The next time you see the ice-cream van, go on treat yourself to a Mr Whippy with strawberry or chocolate sauce. What about a 99 or a waver? – Yummy!

Do you remember the chimes of the ice-cream van as it came along your street and running inside your house to ask your mum for money to buy an ice-cream or ice-lolly?

Hot, sunny days at the beach and standing in the queue looking at the poster in the ice-cream van window trying to decide what you wanted before it was your turn to be served. The ice-cream dribbling onto your hand as it melted in the heat and trying to lick it off before it dribbled down your arm.

Even our dog enjoys a cone or unfinished tub of ice-cream occasionally.

"The art of being happy lies in the power of extracting happiness from common things."

- Henry Ward Beecher

Go to the playpark

"Age is an issue of mind over matter. If
you don't mind, it doesn't matter."
- Mark Twain

The next time you pass a play park go in and have a play, and if
you need to take a child with you so you don't feel silly then go
ahead.

How high can you go on the swing? Go down the chute on your
tummy, head first. Make the roundabout go as fast as you can
and jump on.

How good are you on the monkey bars?

It's a great way to get fresh air and exercise in a fun and
spontaneous way.

Have you noticed in some parks beside the children's play area
adult equipment has been popping up? Supposedly it's for
exercising but they can't kid me there's too much fun and hilarity
going on.

"Happiness is not something readymade. It comes from your own actions."

- Dalai Lama XIV

Buy a toy

"When I am grown to mans estate I shall be
very proud and great. And tell the other girls
and boys not to meddle with my toys."
- Robert Louis Stevenson

Go to a toy shop and have fun looking around. See if you can
find your favourite toys from your childhood. Is there a toy
you wanted as a child but didn't get? What about a toy you
particularly enjoyed playing with as a child.

Whatever toy you choose just make sure you play with it when
you get home.

I bought a clay modelling kit and my husband bought an Airfix
model aeroplane kit and we spent a rainy Sunday afternoon
sitting at the kitchen table making our models.

Phil's spitfire is now on display in our son's bedroom but my
effort I'm sorry to say was only fit for the bin. Still, if at first you
don't succeed.......

"Life begins as a quest of the child for the man and ends as a journey by the man to rediscover the child."

- Lauren Van der Post

Have a water pistol fight

"With mirth and laughter let old wrinkles come."
— William Shakespeare

Do you remember on those hot summer days having water pistol fights with your friends? Throwing water balloons at each other? Playing in teams and hiding from each other ready to jump out and shoot?

Your mum shouting at you for everyone filling their gun or balloon from your kitchen tap and trailing water through the house. Walking home soaking wet with your clothes sticking to you?

Get some friends round or ask the kids if you can join in their game. Wear old clothes; don't have had your hair recently done and take of your mascara. Also don't trust those pesky kids as they have a habit of ganging up on the adults.

"You will find more happiness growing down than up"

~ Author Unknown

Look at the stars

"If the stars should appear but one night every
thousand years how man would marvel and stare."
- Ralph Waldo Emerson

Go outside tonight; look at the sky and say;

"Starlight, star bright,
the first star I see tonight
I wish I may, I wish I might
have the wish I wish tonight."
- Traditional

Then make your wish.

The next clear night lie on a blanket on the grass and just spend some time looking up at the stars. As your eyes get accustomed to the dark, more and more stars will reveal themselves and you might even see a shooting star.

The stars put on a show for us every night that we sometimes take them for granted but just looking up and acknowledging their beauty and the vastness of the Universe can't help but touch a place in your heart.

When my mother-in-law died we decided, as a way of remembering her, to get a star named after her. We got it in a gift box with details of where her star is located and the best time of the year to see the star from earth.

So up there in the sky is a star named "The Catherine Moore Star."

"Dwell on the beauty of life. Watch the stars and see yourself running with them."

- Marcus Aurelius

Climb a tree

"If growing up means it would be beneath
my dignity to climb a tree, I'll never grow up,
never grow up, never grow up! Not me!"
- J M Barrie

Choose a big sturdy tree with branches close together and strong enough to hold your weight. Be careful as you climb and remember you've got to get back down. Not only is this good exercise but you'll increase your self-confidence as you do something which is fun and scary at the same time.

Then just sit on a branch, have a rest, relax and feel all the tension release from your body as you connect with nature and survey the landscape around you. Feel at one with the world and forget your cares for a moment.

If the thought of climbing a tree sounds fun but a bit daunting to you then there are also lots of outdoor centres where you can climb trees with ropes and harnesses safely and with supervision.

So, get out of your comfort zone, have some fresh air and exercise.

See what you're made of. Go on I dare you!

"Everybody is a genius. But if you judge a fish by its ability to climb a tree, it will live its whole life believing that it is stupid."

- Albert Einstein

Climb a hill

"It's easier to go down a hill than up it but
the view is much better at the top."
- Henry Ward Beecher

Breathing in all that fresh air, exercising your body, toning and shaping your legs beats going to the gym any day and it's not just about getting to the top but about all the things you'll see on the way, strange rock formations, beautiful wild flowers, lovely scenery.

And when you do get to the top and look around, admiring the view you'll have a great sense of achievement and can say to yourself with pride,

"I did it!"

"Every mountain top is within reach if you just keep climbing."

- Barry Finlay, *Kilimanjaro and Beyond*

Run down a hill

"If you never attempt the ascent, you'll never know
the thrill of swooshing down the other side."
-Author unknown

I always remember being at the top of a large hill and holding my arms out at either side (like an aeroplane) and launching myself into the fastest run I could manage getting faster and faster as I got to the bottom of the hill, not really knowing if I had enough space to stop and feeling that I was taking giant steps!!!

Why did I do this?

Because it's the fastest way to get to the bottom and it's fun and scary at the same time especially when you're going so fast you can't stop.

Go find a hill and be that kid again, or run down a hill racing your children.

If you're a keen runner, incorporating downhill running into your practice can improve your running speed, strength and endurance. Be careful not to do too much too soon, running downhill may take less effort but it can be harder on the body.

"Our greatest glory is not in never falling, but in rising every time we fall."

- Confucius

Grow a plant from seed

"Weeds are flowers too, once you get to know them."
- A.A. Milne

Did you ever eat an apple or orange and plant the seeds to see if they would grow into a tree? What about growing cress seeds on wet cotton wool?

Getting your hands dirty, being in the fresh air and getting close to nature improves your mood and helps you learn patience as you wait for things to grow in their own good time.

You don't even need to have a garden or a window box. Just a pot on the kitchen window ledge will do.

Choose a plant that appeals to your senses. You may like one that looks pretty or smells nice. You may prefer a plant that is prickly to touch or tasty to eat.

There's something about planting a seed and watching a little shoot appear and get taller and stronger every day that brings out the mothering instinct in you. The pride you feel when it blossoms into a beautiful flower.

"Don't judge each day by the harvest you reap but by the seeds that you plant."

- Robert Louis Stevenson

Rock, paper, scissors

"I must have a prodigious amount of mind; it takes
me as much as a week, sometimes, to make it up!"
- Mark Twain

Next time you and your partner can't agree on something, use this method to decide, rock breaks scissors, scissors cut paper and paper covers rock.

Flip a coin.

Do one potato, two potato, three potato, four, five potato, six potato, seven potato more, you are out!

It's harder work not making a decision. You could be letting weeks, months, even years go by while you are still humming and hawing about moving house, changing jobs, getting married. It also gets very boring for friends and families having to constantly listen to your indecisiveness. What if instead of worrying about making the right or wrong choice, you thought that no choice was wrong? What if you made the decision on what made YOU feel happy and never mind about what others thought? What if you decide to go with your gut instinct even though it doesn't make any sense?

Make the decision, leave the other choices behind and make whatever you decided the right one. If you decide to move home then start looking, make an appointment with the bank manager; get your finances in order. If instead you choose to stay then move the furniture around, do some DIY, and love your home.

If you give the choice you made your full focus and it hasn't made you happy then make another choice. It doesn't mean you've failed; it's been a good thing because it's shown you what you really want.

"A person who
never made
a mistake,
never tried
anything new."

- Albert Einstein

Bubbles

"I drink Champagne when I win, to celebrate...
And I drink Champagne when I lose, to console myself."
- Napoleon Bonaparte

Have a bubble bath with lots of bubbles. Stand up and cover yourself in foam. Give yourself a foam hat and a foam beard.

Get a bottle of bubbles and have fun blowing out lots and lots of beautiful bubbles. Try and catch them with your hand or the stick without bursting any.

Chew a big piece of bubble gum and blow a big bubble. Have a competition to see who can blow the biggest bubble and if it looks like someone else is winning pop their bubble with your finger and see it go all over their face.

For something a bit more grown up, treat yourself to a bottle of champagne. You don't need a special occasion you deserve the best just for being you.

"Look within. Within is the fountain of good, and it will ever bubble up, if thou wilt ever dig."

- Marcus Aurelius

Make a den

"When I grow up I want to be a little boy."
- Joseph Heller

Put a bed sheet over some chairs or the kitchen table. Make it comfortable and cosy inside with cushions and rugs, Have a picnic in it, read a book, listen to music or have a nap. Feel safe and cocooned from the outside world for a short time.

If you want, make your den somewhere it can stay up for a while. Put a sign outside saying:

"KEEP OUT!" or "COME IN!"

Make a den outside in the garden or go out into the countryside. Use fallen branches or bamboo poles. Cover with tarpaulin to make a rain proof shelter. Be creative and have fun.

"If you don't build your dream, someone else will hire you to help them build theirs."

- Dhirubhai Amban

Play sevensies

"If you obey all the rules you miss all the fun."
- Katherine Hepburn

This game is played with a tennis ball and I'm sure everyone had their own way of playing sevensies but just in case you've forgotten here are a few suggestions:

Onesies – throw the ball against the wall and catch it before it hits the ground.

Twosies - throw the ball against the wall and let it bounce once on the ground before you catch it

Threesies – throw the ball against the wall and clap your hands under your leg then catch it before it hits the ground.

Foursies – throw the ball against the wall, turn around and catch it before it hits the ground.

Fivesies – throw the ball against the wall and clap your hands behind your back then catch it before it hits the ground.

Sixies – throw the ball against the wall, touch the floor then catch the ball before it hits the ground.

Sevensies - throw the ball under your leg to hit the wall and catch it before it hits the ground.

The goal is to reach the end without having dropped the ball then you can start again but make it harder by doing the actions twice.

"You miss 100% of the shots you don't take."

- Wayne Gretzky

Play with a yo-yo

"If at first you don't succeed, try, try again. Then
quit. No use being a damn fool about it."
- W.C. Fields

Yo-yo's are one of the oldest toys around and are still as popular today with events held all over the world for people to showcase their skills.

They are cheap to buy and small enough for you to carry around in your pocket.

There are lots of easy tricks to learn and once you master the basics you can move onto the more difficult tricks.

You'll need to keep practicing but it's a great confidence booster when you get the hang of a trick that seemed so difficult at first.

"Man often becomes what he believes himself to be. If I keep on saying to myself that I cannot do a certain thing, it is possible that I may end by really becoming incapable of doing it. On the contrary, if I have the belief that I can do it, I shall surely acquire the capacity to do it even if I may not have it at the beginning."

- Mahatma Gandhi

Puzzles

"You can't connect the dots looking forward; you can only
connect them looking backwards. So you have to trust
that the dots will somehow connect in your future."
- Steve Jobs

Buy a puzzle book or do the crossword in the paper.

Doing a puzzle is great exercise for the brain. It keeps the mind
active and may reduce the effects of dementia. Your memory
increases and you improve your vocabulary and spelling abilities.

Who would have thought all this was happening when all you
were doing was sitting quietly doing the puzzles for fun or just
to stop being bored on a long journey.

I used to enjoy joining up the dots. You would have a page of
dots with numbers on that you would draw a line between in
numerical order to make a picture appear. It was like magic as
something recognisable would appear out of nothing.

"Who in the world am I? Ah, that's the great puzzle."

- Lewis Carroll

Do a magic trick

"Any sufficiently advanced technology is
indistinguishable from magic."
- Arthur C. Clarke

Do you remember getting a box of magic tricks at Christmas
then spending the next few days amazing your family with your
magic skills?

You don't even have to buy anything to start doing some magic
as there are plenty of easy tricks that you can do with things
around the house.

The rubber pencil trick – get a normal pencil and hold it between
your thumb and index finger, don't squeeze too hard then just
move it up and down and it'll look like it's made of rubber.

The magnetic pencil trick – get a normal pencil and tell your
audience that you can make this pencil stick to your hand. Hold
the pencil in your fist and grab your wrist with your other hand.
As you do this secretly place your index finger on the pencil.
Slowly lift your fingers to show that the pencil is stuck to your
hand. The audience won't see your finger holding the pencil.

"And above all,
watch with glittering
eyes the whole world
around you because
the greatest secrets
are always hidden
in the most unlikely
places. Those who
don't believe in
magic will never
find it."

- Roald Dahl

Watch the clouds

"A pessimist sees only the dark side of the clouds, and
mopes; a philosopher sees both sides and shrugs; an optimist
doesn't see the clouds at all – he's walking on them."
- Leonard Louis Levinson

How often do we go about our day and just glance up at the sky
to see what the weather's like. Do we need to take an umbrella;
will it be ok to hang our washing out?

Yet there's so much more to looking up and seeing the clouds
roll by.

It's a great stress reliever. Looking out of your window or better
still lying on a blanket on the ground watching the clouds
connects you to nature and the beauty of life. It clears your mind
and may help you get a better perspective of any problems you
may have. You may receive messages from your subconscious
that pop out as inspiration to do something.

Observing the clouds increases your imagination as you make
shapes out of the different formations and it's fun to do by
yourself or with a friend as you agree and disagree about what
shapes you see.

You could even learn what the different clouds mean and predict
the weather for yourself.

"If you have built castles in the air, your work need not be lost; That is where they should be. Now put foundations under them."

- Henry David Thoreau

Go to the swimming pool

"I know it is wet and the sun is not sunny, but we
can have lots of good fun that is funny."
- Dr. Seuss, *the Cat in the Hat*

We all know swimming is good for you but sometimes it can be
a bit boring swimming up and down doing lengths. It's time to
have a bit more fun, so............

Go down the flumes. See how long you can hold your breath
under water. Do somersaults and headstands. How far can you
swim under the water with just one breath? Throw your locker
key (if it's attached to the band) in at the deep end and when it
sinks, dive down and retrieve it. Jump in the deep end. Practice
diving. Get a row from the life guard for dive-bombing.

You get the idea. What did you enjoy doing when you went
swimming as a child? It might even have been getting a sweetie
out of the vending machine afterwards or going to the chip shop
on your way home.

 Anyway, you deserve it after all that exercise!

Our local swimming pool has started night time swimming
sessions where the pool is lit up by beautiful blue and purple
lights. It's very calming and relaxing to swim in when it's dark
outside.

"Don't wait. The time will never be just right."

– Napoleon Hill

Cuddle

"A hug is like a boomerang – you get it back right away."
- Bill Keane

There are so many health benefits to giving and receiving cuddles such as lowering blood pressure, reducing stress, relieving pain and just feeling nice that it might be "a cuddle a day keeps the doctor away."

A cuddle can convey so many things that words can't. It nurtures a warm and loving relationship with your partner, children, family and friends.

In fact never mind one a day try and get as many as you can. If there's no one around, cuddle yourself, wrap your arms around yourself and squeeze. Hug your pet, your teddy bear, or go for a massage.

Now I know that not everyone is touchy, feely, and will find that even the thought of giving someone a cuddle uncomfortable but even a gentle touch of the hand on someone's arm can convey love and empathy.

Go on; see how many cuddles you can give today!

"Being deeply loved by someone gives you strength, while loving someone deeply gives you courage."

- Lao Tzu

Have a sleepover

"Good friends, good books, and a sleepy
conscience: this is the ideal life."
- Mark Twain

Invite over some friends for a pyjama party. You may need to tell
them to bring their own pillow and sleeping bag.

Get in plenty of food and drink. Have lots of good music to listen
to and a selection of films to watch. Play some games, do each
other's hair and nails. Make cocktails and gossip. Play truth or
dare and spin the bottle. Dance and get the karaoke machine out.
Have a midnight feast.

Just make sure you don't have to do anything or be anywhere
the next day.

"Finish each day and be done with it. You have done what you could. Some blunders and absurdities no doubt crept in; forget them as soon as you can. Tomorrow is a new day. You shall begin it serenely and with too high a spirit to be encumbered with your old nonsense."

- Ralph Waldo Emerson

Make a daisy chain

"There are always flowers for those who want to see them."
- Henri Matisse

Sitting on the grass surrounded by daisies on a warm summer day with only the sound of a bird singing in the distance and a bee buzzing nearby brings it home how the simple things in life can be so pleasurable. So relax, chill out and the only thing you need to think about is what daisy you'll pick.

The best daisies to pick are the ones with good long stalks. Make a split about halfway down with your thumbnail big enough to put the stalk of another daisy through. Keep going until you've got enough length to make a necklace or crown for your head.

"It does not matter how slowly you go as long as you do not stop."

- Confucius

Go to the funfair

"Disneyland will never be completed. It will continue to grow as long as there is imagination left in the world."
— Walt Disney Company

Most of us have memories of going to the funfair as a child whether it was to a big theme park, the shows at the seaside or one of the travelling fairs that would come to your local park every summer.

Some were big and exciting while others looked sad and tatty (especially if it was raining). But it was still fun winning a cuddly toy on the shooting range, throwing ping pong balls into goldfish bowls and playing the one-armed bandits.

Then there were the waltzers where you hoped the man would come and spin you faster; the dodgems and the big, well biggish, big wheel.

And what about all the toffee apples, candy floss, striped rock and sugar mice?

So go on. Eat the candyfloss. Ride the ghost train. Get your palm read. Any rides you normally avoid because they are too scary just try, you never know, they might be more fun than you think. It's a way of facing fear and overcoming it in a safe way because no matter how scary the ride is you know it'll be over in a few minutes.

Be brave, be fearless!

"None are so old as those who have outlived enthusiasm."

- Henry David Thoreau

Send yourself to your room

"Better three hours too soon than a minute too late."
- William Shakespeare

The people we tend to get angry with the most are those we love the most. When things have calmed down we feel bad and regret what has been said because we would never want to hurt them.

And harsh words can never be taken back.

What's more important to be right or to be happy?

The next time you feel your temper rising and before the red mist descends give yourself some time out and go to your room. Punch the pillow if you have to, take deep breaths, read a book, have a nap. Do whatever it takes to distract yourself. Don't go over the old hurts you'll only find more reasons to justify why you have every right to feel that way.

When you've calmed down no matter the rights or wrongs remember the reasons you love that person, what's good about them, why you like being with them. And when you can think about that person without feeling anger or resentment then let yourself out, or if you're enjoying the peace and quiet stay there for a bit longer and just chill.

"For every minute you are angry you lose sixty seconds of happiness."

- Ralph Waldo Emerson

Ask questions

"Sometimes the questions are complicated
and the answers are simple."
- Dr. Seuss

We ask questions all day everyday whether it's to another person or that little voice inside our head. As small children we were constantly asking questions. "Why is the grass green? Where do babies come from? Why does that man have no hair?

But are we asking the right questions? Are we asking ourselves questions that are empowering us or disempowering us? One way to know is by how it feels when you ask the question. If you feel anything other than good then you're on the wrong track. Say you could do with having more money in your life, what questions do you ask yourself?

"Why have I got no money? Where does all my money go? Why do they have money and I don't?" - Doesn't feel very good.

Or

"How can I have money come to me easily?" "What can I do to make sure I have more money coming in than going out?" "How can I become as rich as them?" - Feels a bit better.

Or

"Why does money come to me easily?" "Why am I so good at managing my money?" "Why am I rich in so many ways?" - Feels great.

When you ask yourself empowering questions something shifts in your consciousness. It might not happen right away but by asking the right questions you'll at least feel a hell of a lot better. Try it and see what happens!

"He who has a why to live for can bear almost any how."

- Friedrich Nietzsche

Have a reward chart

"Self confidence is the most attractive quality
a person can have. How can anyone see how
awesome you are if you can't see it yourself."
Author unknown

We all need a bit of praise and encouragement to motivate us to keep going with our goals and there's nothing that our inner child appreciates more than lots of bright, colourful stickers.

If you're feeling arty then make your own reward chart otherwise they are easily bought from local shops, you could download one from various sites online or just use an everyday calendar.

If you're not a sticker person then what about using an empty jam jar and every time you want to reward yourself, stick a marble in.

And when the jam jar is full of marbles or you have lots of lovely stickers then make sure you give yourself a great big treat. You deserve it!

My husband and I each have a wall planner that we put little stickers on each time we've done some exercise. We use a blue dot for running, red dot for walking, yellow dot for yoga and so on. It's a good way to see how much or how little exercise we're doing especially if it's on the lead up to our holidays.

"The starting point of all achievement is desire."

- Napoleon Hill

Have a role model

"Nothing can stop the man with the right mental attitude from achieving his goal; nothing on earth can help the man with the wrong mental attitude."
Thomas Jefferson

As children our role models would have been our parents, other family members or teachers. As we got older we may have looked to celebrities or sports stars. A positive role model inspires us to action, shows us what is possible to achieve in our life. You only have to look through history at all the great leaders or ask any successful person and you will find that they all had someone that they looked up to, respected and used as their guide along the way.

Whatever situation you need a role model for, whether it's for being successful in business, sport, and the arts or if you're struggling with life's challenges, it's important that you find a person who has the positive qualities and experience that can encourage you to move forward to greater things in your life.

Read their autobiographies, have their picture somewhere you can see it every day. If you're not sure what to do say to yourself "what would........... do?

"We are what we repeatedly do. Excellence, therefore, is not an act but a habit"

- Aristotle

Love yourself unconditionally

"It ain't what they call you, it's what you answer to."
~W.C. Fields

Children come from a place of self-love. They want to do what makes them happy and feels good. They want to make their own choices and try new things because they're so sure of their own abilities.

Do you still love yourself?

How often do you tell yourself how well you've done, how proud you are of yourself, how good you are looking?

How well do you love your body by eating healthy, nutritious food, exercising and making healthy lifestyle choices?

Do you have people in your life who adore you and love you, who are fun to be with and support you in all that you do?

Are you in a job that you enjoy, working with people who respect your abilities and tell you often how good a job you're doing?

Do you treat yourself often without feeling guilty because you know you deserve the best?

If you find it difficult to love yourself unconditionally whatever the reason then you may be able to find it for that little child within you. Find a picture of yourself at about age 3 or 4. Look at the picture and say to that beautiful, precious and perfect child all the things you want to say to yourself but can't. That little child deserves the very best, to know that it is loved and wanted. You deserve it too!

"A man is not old until regrets take the place of dreams."

- John Barrymore

Make friends

"Friendship is born at that moment when one person says
to another: "What! you too? I thought I was the only one."
C.S. Lewis

If only it was as easy as going over and saying "can I play?" but
it is about taking that first step by striking up a conversation
instead of the usual nod of the head and smile, and asking that
mum you talk to in the playground to come round for a coffee.

Is your first reaction when you get an invitation, to say "no, I
can't because..." and reel of a list of excuses.

Well, you could be missing out on all sorts of ways of having fun
and meeting people. Doors open in places you least expect them.
For all you know the Universe might have Mr or Miss Right all
lined up and ready to go but you keep turning down offers to go
to places and events where they'll be.

We humans are sociable by nature and yes it is nice to spend some
time alone but as children we instinctively knew the importance
of having someone to play with. We enjoyed playing with our
friends, running round to their house after tea to see if they were
coming out to play and hating it when your mum called you in
at night while you were still playing your game, "just 5 more
minutes, pleeeease?"

"Success is not final, failure is not fatal: it is the courage to continue that counts."

- Winston Churchill

Paper fortune teller

"A child of five would understand this. Send
someone to fetch a child of five."
- Groucho Marx

If you've never made one before or can't remember how to I've tried to make the instructions as simple as possible. I know it's always better if someone can show you and again the good old internet has lots of sites with clear instructions and videos you can follow.

If you haven't got a square piece of paper then get a sheet of A4, take the bottom right hand corner and fold it over to make a triangle. Cut off the rectangle piece that you have left then open the paper up and you should have a square.

Take the top right corner and fold it over to the bottom left corner to make a triangle then take the top left corner down to the bottom right corner to make a smaller triangle.

Open the paper up and place it on the table as a diamond shape. Take the right point and place it in the middle, the left point and place it in the middle, top point then bottom point into the middle and you should have a square shape.

Turn it over and place on the table as a diamond shape then repeat, right corner into centre, then left, top and bottom.

Lift it off the table and put your thumbs and forefingers into the flaps underneath. Pinch your thumb and forefinger on your right hand together and your thumb and forefinger on your left hand together at the same time. Open the flaps by separating your thumbs and fingers then pinch them back again. Keeping the thumb and fingers pinched pull the flaps apart.

On the outer four flaps write a different colour on each one and colour it in if you want. On the inside you have four flaps split down the middle to make eight. On each of these write a number 1 – 8 and under each number write a fortune. "You look beautiful/handsome today" or "you will receive a surprise gift, good news, money." Have some fun with it.

Have the person whose fortune you are telling pick one of the colours on the flaps then move the flaps for each letter. They then have a choice of four numbers and you move the flaps that many times. They pick a number again and this time you open the flap and reveal their fortune.

"The future depends on what you do today."

- Mahatma Gandhi

Befriend a pet

"Dogs have masters. Cats have staff."
Anonymous

Most of us at sometime in our childhood would have pestered our parents for a pet. Maybe you were lucky enough to finally wear them down with your constant asking and promises of how you would do all the work involved. (Hands up, how long did that last!)

Having a pet in our life to look after, play with and stroke, who gives us unconditional love and friendship, who we can talk to and who listens without judgement is a bonus in anyone's life.

I know we all haven't got the time or the inclination to care for a pet full time and they are a big responsibility, but we can sometimes enjoy the companionship they provide.

Maybe you have a friend or neighbour who needs help with their pet?

They may be going on holiday or into hospital, they might simply have to work late one night and you could offer to feed their cat or walk their dog.

Animals do so much for us and are so easy to love why not give something back and sponsor an animal from the local animal shelter or even pop in some tins of food.

"Until one has loved an animal, a part of one's soul remains unawakened."

- Anatole France

Day out

"Don't cry because it's over, smile because it happened."
- Dr Seuss

Visit the Zoo and take a picnic. Make sure you go to the souvenir shop on the way out and buy yourself a gift to remind yourself of your trip.

Go to a petting farm and feed the animals. They sometimes have sessions where you can hold the animals. It might be a cute bunny rabbit or baby chick, maybe even something more exotic like a tarantula or meerkat.

Is there a museum you haven't visited yet? Or one you haven't been to since you were a child? Check out any special exhibitions or talks that are being held and spend a relaxing afternoon wandering around looking at the exhibits and going to the coffee shop.

Instead of jumping in the car take the bus or go by train and visit a nearby town that you don't know very well.

I used to spend a lot of rainy Sunday afternoons as a child going round the museum. I loved pressing buttons to make lights go on and wheels turn and my favourite section was the dinosaur and Egyptian exhibits.

"The journey of a thousand miles begins with a single step."

- Lao Tzu

Tidy your room

"Excuse the mess, but we live here."
- Roseanne Barr

"TIDY YOUR ROOM!" How many times did you hear that growing up? But there comes a time when you decide you're going to de-clutter, either because you're fed up living with the mess or you've heard that getting rid of the old makes space for the new in your life. Out with all that old, stagnant energy and in with the new fresh energy.

Getting started is normally always the hardest part, so to get into the right frame of mind, a day or two before you start, go into the room you're going to organize a couple of times and picture what it will look like when you're finished and how pleased with yourself you'll be. Really feel that sense of achievement of a job well done. Think about what you'll need for storage and whether or not you'll need to buy anything so that you have everything you need on the day. It means that when you start to tidy for real you'll have a better idea of where you want things to go and it doesn't seem so overwhelming.

Then when you're all done and standing back admiring your work, think back to how you had wanted to feel at this point. "I DID IT"

Doing this actually gets me looking forward to doing the work and I seem to get it done quicker, with less hassle and it's more enjoyable.

"Out of clutter,
find simplicity.
From discord,
find harmony.
In the middle
of difficulty lies
opportunity."

- Albert Einstein

Write a letter

"I have only made this letter longer because I
have not had the time to make it shorter."
Blaise Pascal

Did you have a post office set or a fancy box with drawers that you pulled out with coloured paper and envelopes inside? What about a special pen or pencil? Maybe you had a favourite pencil topper of a monster, troll or funny animal?

Buy a pretty stationery set or some nice paper and write a letter to someone. It could be a thank you letter for a lovely present or day out. A letter to someone you have lost touch with or a love letter. You could decorate with stickers or draw some doodles to personalise it. Spray perfume on the envelope and kiss the envelope before you send it.

Whose face doesn't light up when they receive a handwritten envelope through the post from someone they care about? It makes you feel connected to the person who sent it. You can physically hold something they held close to your heart and have as a lovely memory keepsake that you can look at again and again.

You could write a letter to the universe thanking the universe for all the wonderful things in your life. It might be gratitude for what you have now or what you're wishing for. "Thank you for my beautiful home near the sea, my fantastic sports car sitting in the garage, the lovely holiday to my dream destination." Have fun with it then put the letter in a drawer and forget about it for a while. You might be surprised when you look at it at a later date!

Writing down your thoughts, especially painful ones can help release the intensity of those feelings. Don't keep them bottled up; write down everything that comes up, not stopping until you've said everything you wanted to say. The release of all that emotion should make you feel a lot better.

Then destroy the letter!

"Everything we hear is an opinion, not a fact. Everything we see is a perspective, not the truth."

- Marcus Aurelius

Keep a diary

"I never travel without my diary. One should always
have something sensational to read on the train."
Oscar Wilde

How often did you get a new fresh diary at the beginning of the
year? Did you have a secret hiding place for it or did it have a lock
and key so no-one could open it up and look at all your secrets.

I'd love to say that I wrote in my diary faithfully every day, and
I'm sure like a lot of people I started off with that intention, but
over the weeks it seemed like I was writing the same things all
the time and it became boring. It ended up being more like a
weather report. "Sunny today or it's still raining."

Still it is fun to find an old diary and look back at things you had
forgotten. Boys you fancied, arguments with your parents, places
you went with friends.

You don't need to buy an actual diary; you could use a notebook
or journal and write in the dates. That way you don't have to write
every day, it may only be once a week or at the weekend.

I keep a fun diary that I write in every day so that I make sure I do
at least one fun activity every day. It doesn't have to be anything
big just spending five minutes watching animals doing funny
things on you-tube, dancing to a song or going to the beach.
Little things that make me feel good like my son holding my
hand or receiving a compliment. As I look back I'll realise that
as I've already quoted, that the little things were the important
things.

"The life of every man is a diary in which he means to write one story, and writes another; and his humblest hour is when he compares the volume as it is with what he vowed to make it."

- James M. Barrie

"Do you think I've gone round the bend?" "I'm afraid so. You're mad, bonkers, completely off your head. But I'll tell you a secret. All the best people are."

- Lewis Carroll, Alice in Wonderland

"And in the end it is not the years in your life that count, it's the life in your years."

- Abraham Lincoln